HEAR THE WORD

A Sermon Activity Book

GOSPEL GROWN

Louisville, Kentucky

Hear the Word: A Sermon Activity Book

Cover Image by Hayley Krahwinkle
Interior Images by Lindsey Jacobs

Published by
Gospel Grown
Louisville, KY
www.gospelgrown.org

ISBN: 978-1-7336615-0-8

My name is _____.

I am _____ years old.

I go to _____.
(name of church)

How to Use this Book

Jesus welcomed the little children to come to him and stated that "to such belongs the kingdom of heaven" (Matt 19:14). Paul addressed children directly with his letters assuming they would be present while his letters were read to the churches (Eph 6:1).

Most parents, as their newborn grows into a toddler, will have experienced the difficulty of getting their child to sit still and quietly throughout a sermon. This is often achieved with captivating them with books—whether picture, coloring, or activity books. Most parents also desire, much later, for their child to be able to engage a sermon by listening well and possibly taking notes. But how do you get a toddler to progress from merely sitting still to becoming an active listener who can then take notes? *Hear the Word* is designed to be a tool for these in-between years to help bridge that gap.

Hear the Word was created for children who range from a non-writers to early writers, or age three and older.

There are two aims behind this activity book. The first and foremost is to help young children learn to listen to—and respond to—a sermon. The second aim is to introduce and/or help young children to become familiar with the content and form of a Bible.

There are 52, two-paged activity sheets intended to cover an entire year.

The first page of each activity sheet contains images that relate to a common biblical word that are to be colored when the child hears the word during a sermon.[1] Additionally, the first page contains a phrase to be traced by the child and also a question with a Scripture reference to find the answer.

The second page contains a place for a child to identify the testament, book, chapter and verse(s) of the sermon.[2] Additionally, the second page contains a box for a child to draw a picture inside. The idea is for them to draw a picture of what they determine ought to be their response to hearing God's Word.

---

[1] Without knowing the sermon ahead of time, we have attempted to choose those common biblical words that are expected to appear in most/all sermons. However, there is the real chance that an expected "common" word, does not appear regularly in a particular sermon. If/when this occurs, it is recommended to choose a regularly occurring word for that particular sermon, though obviously it may/will not correspond to the given image.

[2] Children who cannot write will either simply skip this page or need their parents/caregivers to write the answer for them to trace or copy.

This first aim above—teaching children to listen—is accomplished through the coloring images and the place to draw their response. The second aim—teaching familiarity with the Bible—is accomplished through identifying the location of the sermon in a Bible, and looking up the answer to the question.

Paul wrote "...faith comes from hearing, and hearing through the word of Christ" (Romans 10:17). It is our desire that this book will help children hear, and then love God's Word as it transforms their lives.

JESUS IS KING

Listen for the word "Jesus" and color a crown when you hear it:

How many times did you hear "Jesus"? _____

Trace the

sentence:

Talk about it: What kingdom does Jesus rule over?

Look up: John 18:36

WHERE IN THE BIBLE?

1. Circle the testament which the sermon was from:

   OLD TESTAMENT   NEW TESTAMENT

2. What book of the Bible was the sermon from?

   BOOK: _____

3. What chapter and verse was the sermon from?

   CHAPTER: _____   VERSES: _____ — _____

4. Draw a picture of something you need to do to obey God's Word:

ALL PEOPLE SIN

Listen for the word "sin" and color an X when you hear it:

How many times did you hear "sin"? _____

Trace the

sentence:

Talk about it: Why do people sin?

Look up: John 8:34

WHERE IN THE BIBLE?

1. Circle the testament which the sermon was from:

   OLD TESTAMENT   NEW TESTAMENT

2. What book of the Bible was the sermon from?

   BOOK: _____

3. What chapter and verse was the sermon from?

   CHAPTER: _____   VERSES: _____ — _____

4. Draw a picture of something you need to do to obey God's Word:

THE BIBLE IS SHARPER THAN A SWORD

Listen for the word "Bible" and color a Bible when you hear it:

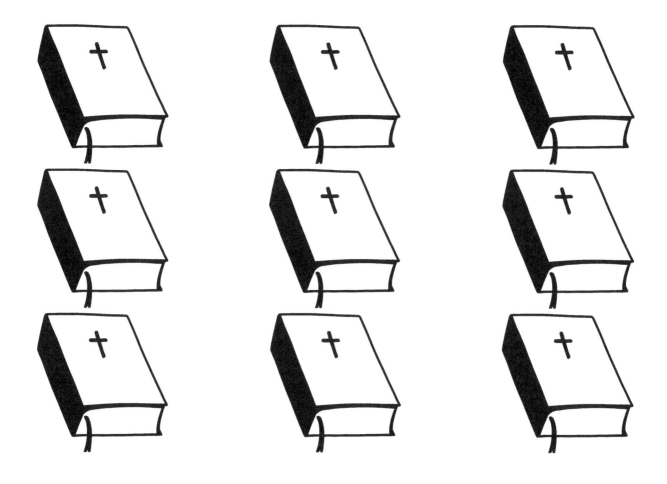

How many times did you hear "Bible"? _____

Trace the

sentence:

Talk about it: How is the Bible like a sword?

Look up: Hebrews 4:12

WHERE IN THE BIBLE?

1. Circle the testament which the sermon was from:

OLD TESTAMENT   NEW TESTAMENT

2. What book of the Bible was the sermon from?

BOOK: _____

3. What chapter and verse was the sermon from?

CHAPTER: _____   VERSES: _____ — _____

4. Draw a picture of something you need to do to obey God's Word:

GOD IS LOVE

Listen for the word "God" and color a trinity symbol when you hear it:

How many times did you hear "God"? _____

Trace the
sentence:

Talk about it: How do we know God is love?

Look up: 1 John 4:8-10

WHERE IN THE BIBLE?

1. Circle the testament which the sermon was from:

OLD TESTAMENT   NEW TESTAMENT

2. What book of the Bible was the sermon from?

BOOK: _____

3. What chapter and verse was the sermon from?

CHAPTER: _____   VERSES: _____ — _____

4. Draw a picture of something you need to do to obey God's Word:

WEEK 5

THE CHURCH IS GOD'S FAMILY

Listen for the words "church" and "God" and color

the right image when you hear them:

How many times did you hear "church"? _____   "God"?   _____

Trace the

sentence:

Talk about it: Why is it important for God's people to meet together?

Look up: Hebrews 10:24-25

WHERE IN THE BIBLE?

1. Circle the testament which the sermon was from:

   OLD TESTAMENT   NEW TESTAMENT

2. What book of the Bible was the sermon from?

   BOOK: _____

3. What chapter and verse was the sermon from?

   CHAPTER: _____   VERSES: _____ — _____

4. Draw a picture of something you need to do to obey God's Word:

LOVE YOUR ENEMIES

Listen for the words "love" and "God" and color
the right image when you hear them:

How many times did you hear "love"? _____   "God"? _____

Trace the
sentence:

Talk about it: Who is able to love their enemies? Do you?

Look up: Matthew 5:44-45

WHERE IN THE BIBLE?

1. Circle the testament which the sermon was from:

OLD TESTAMENT   NEW TESTAMENT

2. What book of the Bible was the sermon from?

BOOK: _____

3. What chapter and verse was the sermon from?

CHAPTER: _____   VERSES: _____ — _____

4. Draw a picture of something you need to do to obey God's Word:

TURN AWAY FROM SIN

Listen for the words "repent" and "sin" and color
the right image when you hear them:

How many times did you hear "repent"? _____   "sin"? _____

Trace the
sentence:

Talk about it: What does the word repent mean?

Look up: Acts 3:19

WHERE IN THE BIBLE?

1. Circle the testament which the sermon was from:

OLD TESTAMENT   NEW TESTAMENT

2. What book of the Bible was the sermon from?

BOOK: _____

3. What chapter and verse was the sermon from?

CHAPTER: _____   VERSES: _____ – _____

4. Draw a picture of something you need to do to obey God's Word:

HEAVEN IS FOR CHILDREN

Listen for the words "heaven" and "Jesus" and color

the right image when you hear them:

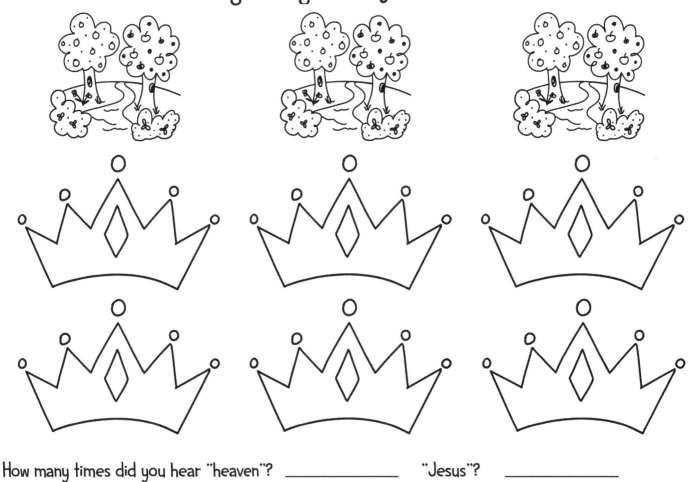

How many times did you hear "heaven"? _____ "Jesus"? _____

Trace the

sentence:

Talk about it: Who said that His kingdom was for children?

Look up: Matthew 19:14

WHERE IN THE BIBLE?

1. Circle the testament which the sermon was from:

    OLD TESTAMENT   NEW TESTAMENT

2. What book of the Bible was the sermon from?

    BOOK: _____

3. What chapter and verse was the sermon from?

    CHAPTER: _____   VERSES: _____ — _____

4. Draw a picture of something you need to do to obey God's Word:

THE WAGES OF SIN IS DEATH

Listen for the words "death" and "sin" and color

the right image when you hear them:

How many times did you hear "death"? _____   "sin"? _____

Trace the

sentence:

Talk about it: Why do people die?

Look up: Romans 5:12

WHERE IN THE BIBLE?

1. Circle the testament which the sermon was from:

OLD TESTAMENT   NEW TESTAMENT

2. What book of the Bible was the sermon from?

BOOK: _____

3. What chapter and verse was the sermon from?

CHAPTER: _____   VERSES: _____ — _____

4. Draw a picture of something you need to do to obey God's Word:

THE HOLY SPIRIT IS A TEACHER

Listen for the words "Spirit" and "God" and color

the right image when you hear them:

How many times did you hear "Spirit"? _____   "God"? _____

Trace the

sentence:

Talk about it: What does the Spirit teach?

Look up: John 14:26

WHERE IN THE BIBLE?

1. Circle the testament which the sermon was from:

   OLD TESTAMENT   NEW TESTAMENT

2. What book of the Bible was the sermon from?

   BOOK: _____

3. What chapter and verse was the sermon from?

   CHAPTER: _____   VERSES: _____ — _____

4. Draw a picture of something you need to do to obey God's Word:

JESUS BEAT SIN

Listen for the words "Jesus" and "sin" and color
the right image when you hear them:

How many times did you hear "Jesus"? _____   "sin"? _____

Trace the
sentence:

Talk about it: How did Jesus beat Sin?

Look up: Romans 6:7

WHERE IN THE BIBLE?

1. Circle the testament which the sermon was from:

   OLD TESTAMENT   NEW TESTAMENT

2. What book of the Bible was the sermon from?

   BOOK: _____

3. What chapter and verse was the sermon from?

   CHAPTER: _____   VERSES: _____ — _____

4. Draw a picture of something you need to do to obey God's Word:

GOD BREATHED OUT THE BIBLE

Listen for the words "God" and "Bible" and color
the right image when you hear them:

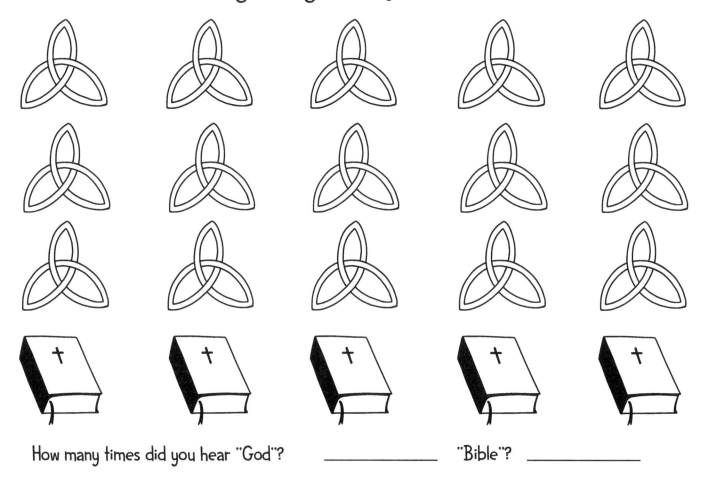

How many times did you hear "God"? _____ "Bible"? _____

Trace the
sentence:

Talk about it: Why should we listen to the Bible?

Look up: 2 Timothy 3:16-17

WHERE IN THE BIBLE?

1. Circle the testament which the sermon was from:

OLD TESTAMENT   NEW TESTAMENT

2. What book of the Bible was the sermon from?

BOOK: _____

3. What chapter and verse was the sermon from?

CHAPTER: _____   VERSES: _____—_____

4. Draw a picture of something you need to do to obey God's Word:

JESUS IS THE HEAD OF THE CHURCH

Listen for the words "Jesus" and "church" and color
the right image when you hear them:

How many times did you hear "Jesus"? _____ "church"? _____

Trace the
sentence:

Talk about it: How is the church like a body?
Look up: 1 Corinthians 12:24-26

WHERE IN THE BIBLE?

1. Circle the testament which the sermon was from:

OLD TESTAMENT   NEW TESTAMENT

2. What book of the Bible was the sermon from?

BOOK: _____

3. What chapter and verse was the sermon from?

CHAPTER: _____   VERSES: _____ — _____

4. Draw a picture of something you need to do to obey God's Word:

THE HOLY SPIRIT LIVES INSIDE GOD'S PEOPLE

Listen for the words "God," "church," and "Holy Spirit" and color
the right image when you hear them:

How many times did you hear "God"? _____ "church"? _____ "Holy Spirit"? _____

Trace the
sentence:

Talk about it: What does the Holy Spirit help God's people do?

Look up: Acts 1:8

WHERE IN THE BIBLE?

1. Circle the testament which the sermon was from:

   OLD TESTAMENT   NEW TESTAMENT

2. What book of the Bible was the sermon from?

   BOOK: _____

3. What chapter and verse was the sermon from?

   CHAPTER: _____   VERSES: _____ – _____

4. Draw a picture of something you need to do to obey God's Word:

THE BIBLE IS LIKE A MIRROR

Listen for the words "Jesus" and "Bible" and color

the right image when you hear them:

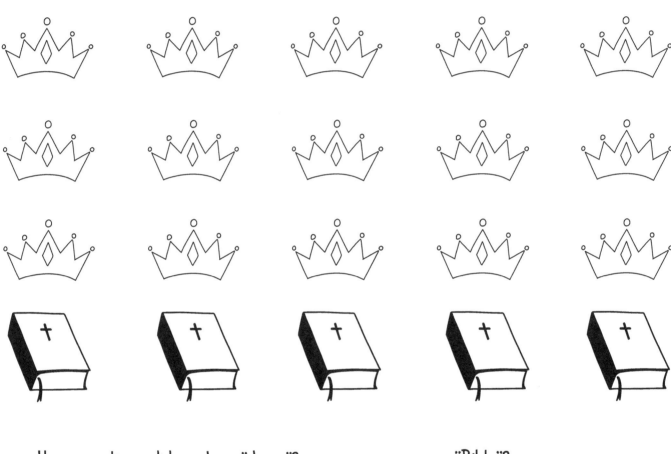

How many times did you hear "Jesus"? _____ "Bible"? _____

Trace the
sentence:

The Bible is like a mirror.

Talk about it: How is the Bible like a mirror?

Look up: James 1:22-25

WHERE IN THE BIBLE?

1. Circle the testament which the sermon was from:

OLD TESTAMENT   NEW TESTAMENT

2. What book of the Bible was the sermon from?

BOOK: _____

3. What chapter and verse was the sermon from?

CHAPTER: _____   VERSES: _____ – _____

4. Draw a picture of something you need to do to obey God's Word:

God's Law is Good

Listen for the words "God" and "Law" and color

the right image when you hear them:

How many times did you hear "God"? _____ "law"? _____

Trace the

sentence:

Talk about it: If God's law is good, why does no-one keep it?

Look up: Romans 7:11-12

WHERE IN THE BIBLE?

1. Circle the testament which the sermon was from:

   OLD TESTAMENT   NEW TESTAMENT

2. What book of the Bible was the sermon from?

   BOOK: _____

3. What chapter and verse was the sermon from?

   CHAPTER: _____   VERSES: _____ − _____

4. Draw a picture of something you need to do to obey God's Word:

JESUS DIED ON THE CROSS

Listen for the words "Jesus" and "cross" and color

the right image when you hear them:

How many times did you hear "Jesus"? _____ "cross"? _____

Trace the
sentence:

Talk about it: Why did Jesus die on the cross?

Look up: 1 Peter 2:24

WHERE IN THE BIBLE?

1. Circle the testament which the sermon was from:

OLD TESTAMENT   NEW TESTAMENT

2. What book of the Bible was the sermon from?

BOOK: _____

3. What chapter and verse was the sermon from?

CHAPTER: _____   VERSES: _____ — _____

4. Draw a picture of something you need to do to obey God's Word:

JESUS IS MAKING A NEW WORLD

Listen for the words "Jesus" and "heaven" and color

the right image when you hear them:

How many times did you hear "Jesus"? _____ "heaven"? _____

Trace the

sentence:

Talk about it: Who is Jesus making a new world for?

Look up: John 14:3-6

WHERE IN THE BIBLE?

1. Circle the testament which the sermon was from:

   OLD TESTAMENT   NEW TESTAMENT

2. What book of the Bible was the sermon from?

   BOOK: _____

3. What chapter and verse was the sermon from?

   CHAPTER: _____   VERSES: _____ – _____

4. Draw a picture of something you need to do to obey God's Word:

WEEK 19

YOU CANNOT LOVE GOD AND MONEY

Listen for the words "God" and "love" and color
the right image when you hear them:

How many times did you hear "God"? _____ "love"? _____

Trace the
sentence:

Talk about it: How do you know what you love the most?
Look up: Matthew 6:21

WHERE IN THE BIBLE?

1. Circle the testament which the sermon was from:

OLD TESTAMENT   NEW TESTAMENT

2. What book of the Bible was the sermon from?

BOOK: _____

3. What chapter and verse was the sermon from?

CHAPTER: _____   VERSES: _____ − _____

4. Draw a picture of something you need to do to obey God's Word:

THE POWER OF SIN IS THE LAW

Listen for the words "Sin" and "Law" and color

the right image when you hear them:

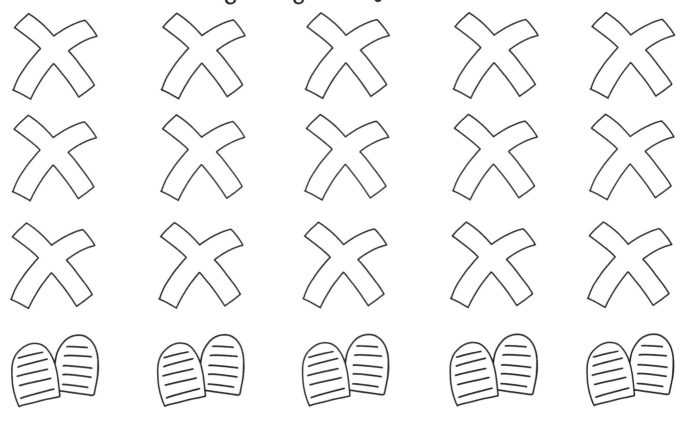

How many times did you hear "Sin"? _____ "Law"? _____

Trace the
sentence:

Talk about it: How does Sin get its strength from the Law?

Look up: Romans 7:7-11

WHERE IN THE BIBLE?

1. Circle the testament which the sermon was from:

OLD TESTAMENT   NEW TESTAMENT

2. What book of the Bible was the sermon from?

BOOK: _____

3. What chapter and verse was the sermon from?

CHAPTER: _____   VERSES: _____ – _____

4. Draw a picture of something you need to do to obey God's Word:

JESUS BAPTIZES WITH THE HOLY SPIRIT

Listen for the words "Jesus" and "Holy Spirit" and color
the right image when you hear them:

How many times did you hear "Jesus"? _____ "Holy Spirit"? _____

Trace the
sentence:

Talk about it: Jesus baptizes with the Holy Spirit and what else?
Look up: Matthew 3:11

WHERE IN THE BIBLE?

1. Circle the testament which the sermon was from:

   OLD TESTAMENT   NEW TESTAMENT

2. What book of the Bible was the sermon from?

   BOOK: _____

3. What chapter and verse was the sermon from?

   CHAPTER: _____   VERSES: _____ — _____

4. Draw a picture of something you need to do to obey God's Word:

GOD SENT JESUS TO SAVE THE WORLD

Listen for the words "God," "Jesus," and "heaven" and color

the right image when you hear them:

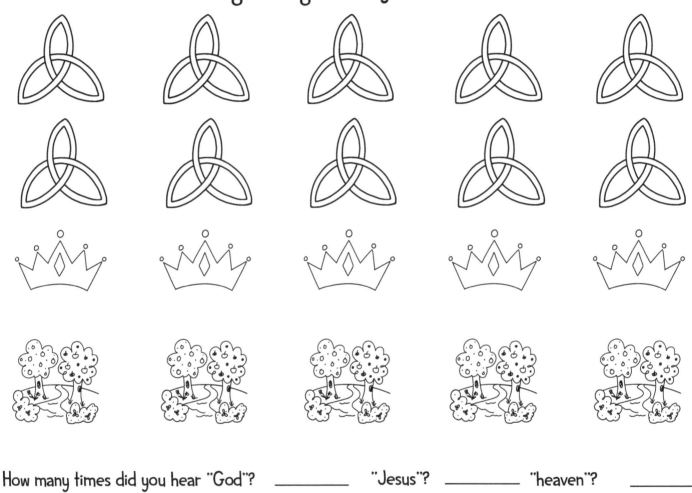

How many times did you hear "God"? _____ "Jesus"? _____ "heaven"? _____

Trace the
sentence:

Talk about it: Why did God send Jesus to save the world?

Look up: John 3:16

WHERE IN THE BIBLE?

1. Circle the testament which the sermon was from:

    OLD TESTAMENT   NEW TESTAMENT

2. What book of the Bible was the sermon from?

    BOOK: _____

3. What chapter and verse was the sermon from?

    CHAPTER: _____   VERSES: _____ — _____

4. Draw a picture of something you need to do to obey God's Word:

GOD IN THREE PERSONS

Listen for the words "God," "Jesus," and "Holy Spirit" and color
the right image when you hear them:

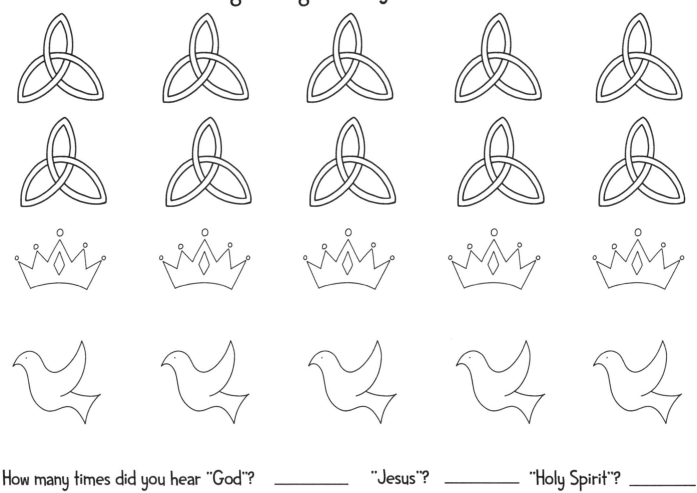

How many times did you hear "God"? _____ "Jesus"? _____ "Holy Spirit"? _____

Trace the
sentence:

Talk about it: Who are the three persons of the trinity?
Look up: 2 Corinthians 13:12

WHERE IN THE BIBLE?

1. Circle the testament which the sermon was from:

   OLD TESTAMENT   NEW TESTAMENT

2. What book of the Bible was the sermon from?

   BOOK: _____

3. What chapter and verse was the sermon from?

   CHAPTER: _____   VERSES: _____ — _____

4. Draw a picture of something you need to do to obey God's Word:

The Spirit Convicts the World about Sin

Listen for the words "Holy Spirit," and "sin" and color
the right image when you hear them:

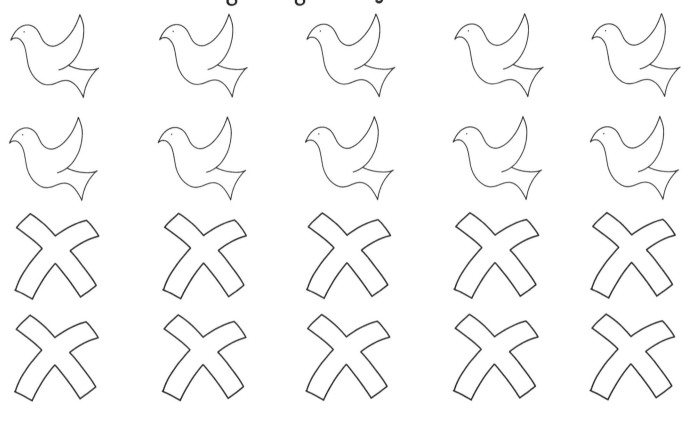

How many times did you hear "Holy Spirit"? _____ "sin"? _____

Trace the
sentence:

Talk about it: Why does the Spirit convinct the world?
Look up: John 16:8-9

WHERE IN THE BIBLE?

1. Circle the testament which the sermon was from:

   OLD TESTAMENT   NEW TESTAMENT

2. What book of the Bible was the sermon from?

   BOOK: _____

3. What chapter and verse was the sermon from?

   CHAPTER: _____   VERSES: _____ − _____

4. Draw a picture of something you need to do to obey God's Word:

JESUS IS THE LAMB OF GOD

Listen for the words "Jesus," "God," and "cross" and color
the right image when you hear them:

How many times did you hear "Jesus"? _____ "God"? _____ "cross"? _____

Trace the
sentence:

Jesus is the lamb of God.

Talk about it: Why is Jesus called a lamb?

Look up: John 1:29

WHERE IN THE BIBLE?

1. Circle the testament which the sermon was from:

    OLD TESTAMENT   NEW TESTAMENT

2. What book of the Bible was the sermon from?

    BOOK: _____

3. What chapter and verse was the sermon from?

    CHAPTER: _____   VERSES: _____ — _____

4. Draw a picture of something you need to do to obey God's Word:

GOD'S PEOPLE LOVE EACH OTHER

Listen for the words "God," "love," and "church" and color

the right image when you hear them:

How many times did you hear "God"? _____   "love"? _____   "church"? _____

Trace the

sentence:

Talk about it: What happens when God's people love each other?

Look up: John 13:34

WHERE IN THE BIBLE?

1. Circle the testament which the sermon was from:

    OLD TESTAMENT   NEW TESTAMENT

2. What book of the Bible was the sermon from?

    BOOK: _____

3. What chapter and verse was the sermon from?

    CHAPTER: _____   VERSES: _____ − _____

4. Draw a picture of something you need to do to obey God's Word:

GOD'S KINGDOM IS NEAR

Listen for the words "God," "sin," and "repent" and color

the right image when you hear them:

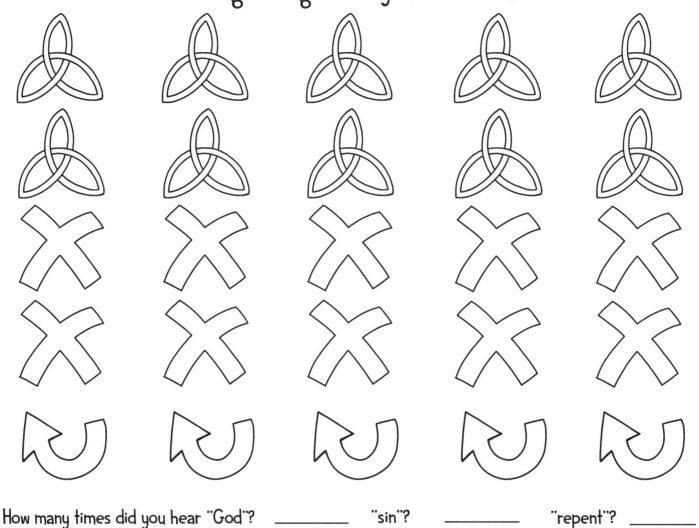

How many times did you hear "God"? _____ "sin"? _____ "repent"? _____

Trace the

sentence:

Talk about it: What should people do because God's kingdom is near?

Look up: Mark 1:15

WHERE IN THE BIBLE?

1. Circle the testament which the sermon was from:

OLD TESTAMENT   NEW TESTAMENT

2. What book of the Bible was the sermon from?

BOOK: _____

3. What chapter and verse was the sermon from?

CHAPTER: _____   VERSES: _____ — _____

4. Draw a picture of something you need to do to obey God's Word:

JESUS BECAME SIN

Listen for the words "Jesus" and "sin" and color

the right image when you hear them:

How many times did you hear "Jesus"? _____ "sin"? _____

Trace the

sentence:

Talk about it: Why did Jesus become sin?

Look up: 2 Corinthians 5:21

WHERE IN THE BIBLE?

1. Circle the testament which the sermon was from:

   OLD TESTAMENT   NEW TESTAMENT

2. What book of the Bible was the sermon from?

   BOOK: _____

3. What chapter and verse was the sermon from?

   CHAPTER: _____   VERSES: _____

4. Draw a picture of something you need to do to obey God's Word:

JESUS HAS THE KEYS OF DEATH

Listen for the words "Jesus" and "death" and color
the right image when you hear them:

How many times did you hear "Jesus"? _____   "death"? _____

Trace the

sentence:

Talk about it: Why does Jesus have the keys of death?

Look up: Revelation 1:18

WHERE IN THE BIBLE?

1. Circle the testament which the sermon was from:

   OLD TESTAMENT   NEW TESTAMENT

2. What book of the Bible was the sermon from?

   BOOK: _____

3. What chapter and verse was the sermon from?

   CHAPTER: _____   VERSES: _____ ‒ _____

4. Draw a picture of something you need to do to obey God's Word:

God Commands All People to Repent

Listen for the words "God" and "repent" and color
the right image when hear them:

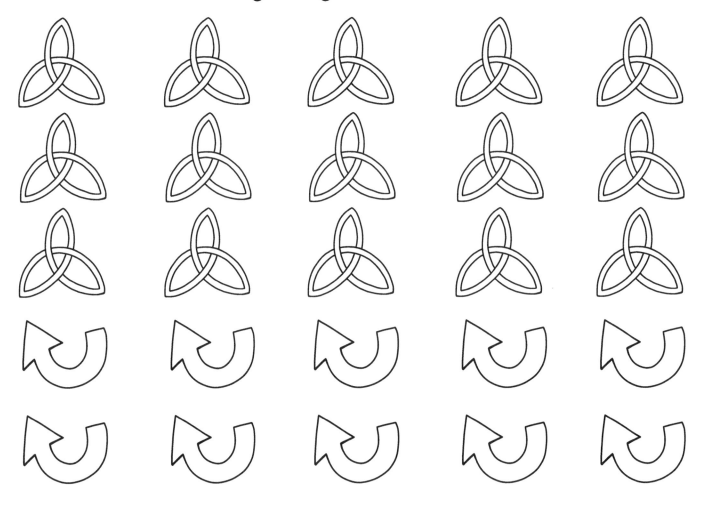

How many times did you hear "God"? _____ "repent"? _____

Trace the
sentence:

Talk about it: Why do we need to repent?

Look up: Acts 17:30–31

WHERE IN THE BIBLE?

1. Circle the testament which the sermon was from:

   OLD TESTAMENT   NEW TESTAMENT

2. What book of the Bible was the sermon from?

   BOOK: _____

3. What chapter and verse was the sermon from?

   CHAPTER: _____   VERSES: _____ — _____

4. Draw a picture of something you need to do to obey God's Word:

Repent for the Forgiveness of Sin

Listen for the words "Jesus," "sin," and "repent" and color
the right image when you hear them:

How many times did you hear "Jesus"? _____   "sin"? _____   "repent"? _____

**Trace the
sentence:**

Talk about it: What will happen if we repent?

Look up: Acts 2:38

WHERE IN THE BIBLE?

1. Circle the testament which the sermon was from:

   OLD TESTAMENT   NEW TESTAMENT

2. What book of the Bible was the sermon from?

   BOOK: _____

3. What chapter and verse was the sermon from?

   CHAPTER: _____   VERSES: _____ — _____

4. Draw a picture of something you need to do to obey God's Word:

JESUS CAME TO FULFILL THE LAW

Listen for the words "Jesus," "law" and color
the right image when you hear them:

How many times did you hear "Jesus"? _____   "law"?   _____

Trace the
sentence:

Talk about it: How can God's people fulfill the law?

Look up: Romans 8:3-4

WHERE IN THE BIBLE?

1. Circle the testament which the sermon was from:

   OLD TESTAMENT   NEW TESTAMENT

2. What book of the Bible was the sermon from?

   BOOK: _____

3. What chapter and verse was the sermon from?

   CHAPTER: _____   VERSES: _____ — _____

4. Draw a picture of something you need to do to obey God's Word:

GOD WRITES HIS LAW ON HIS PEOPLE'S HEARTS

Listen for the words "God," "law," and "church" and color

the right image when you hear them:

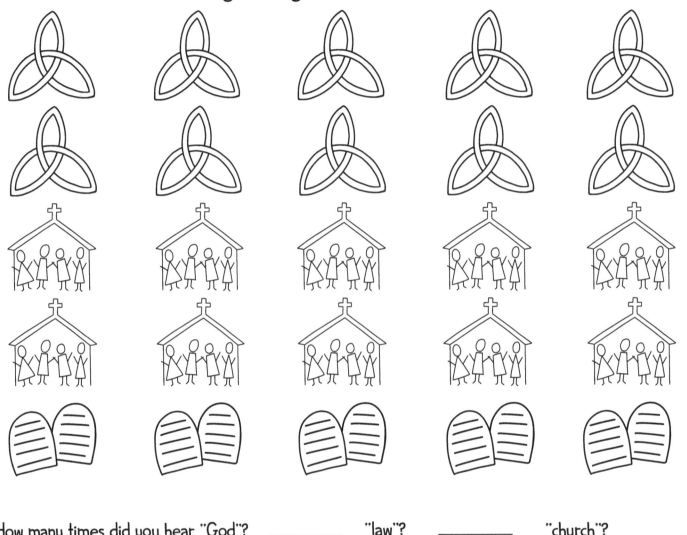

How many times did you hear "God"? _____ "law"? _____ "church"? _____

Trace the

sentence:

Talk about it: What does it means for God to write His law on your heart?

Look up: Jeremiah 31:31-34

WHERE IN THE BIBLE?

1. Circle the testament which the sermon was from:

   OLD TESTAMENT   NEW TESTAMENT

2. What book of the Bible was the sermon from?

   BOOK: _____

3. What chapter and verse was the sermon from?

   CHAPTER: _____   VERSES: _____ — _____

4. Draw a picture of something you need to do to obey God's Word:

JESUS WAS BORN
BY THE HOLY SPIRIT

Listen for the words "Jesus" and "Holy Spirit" and color

the right image when you hear them:

How many times did you hear "Jesus"? _____   "Holy Spirit"? _____

Trace the

sentence:

Talk about it: What was Jesus born to do?

Look up: Matthew 1:21

WHERE IN THE BIBLE?

1. Circle the testament which the sermon was from:

OLD TESTAMENT   NEW TESTAMENT

2. What book of the Bible was the sermon from?

BOOK: _____

3. What chapter and verse was the sermon from?

CHAPTER: _____   VERSES: _____ — _____

4. Draw a picture of something you need to do to obey God's Word:

God Can
Take Away our Sin

Listen for the words "God" and "sin" and color

the right image when you hear them:

How many times did you hear "God"? _____   "sin"? _____

Trace the

sentence:

Talk about it: How far away does God take our sin?

Look up: Psalm 103:12

WHERE IN THE BIBLE?

1. Circle the testament which the sermon was from:

OLD TESTAMENT   NEW TESTAMENT

2. What book of the Bible was the sermon from?

BOOK: _____

3. What chapter and verse was the sermon from?

CHAPTER: _____   VERSES: _____ — _____

4. Draw a picture of something you need to do to obey God's Word:

WHEN WE DIE WE WILL STAND BEFORE GOD

Listen for the words "God" and "death" and color

the right image when you hear them:

How many times did you hear "God"? _____   "death"? _____

Trace the

sentence:

Talk about it: What happens when we die?

Look up: Hebrews 9 :27

WHERE IN THE BIBLE?

1. Circle the testament which the sermon was from:

   OLD TESTAMENT   NEW TESTAMENT

2. What book of the Bible was the sermon from?

   BOOK: _____

3. What chapter and verse was the sermon from?

   CHAPTER: _____   VERSES: _____ — _____

4. Draw a picture of something you need to do to obey God's Word:

Love Your Neighbor as Yourself

Listen for the words "love," "church," "Jesus" and color
the right image when you hear them:

How many times did you hear "love"? _____   "church"? _____   "Jesus"? _____

Trace the

sentence:

Talk about it: Who is your neighbor?

Look up: Luke 10:25-37

WHERE IN THE BIBLE?

1. Circle the testament which the sermon was from:

    OLD TESTAMENT   NEW TESTAMENT

2. What book of the Bible was the sermon from?

    BOOK: _____

3. What chapter and verse was the sermon from?

    CHAPTER: _____   VERSES: _____ ― _____

4. Draw a picture of something you need to do to obey God's Word:

There is no Sin or Death in Heaven

Listen for the words "Jesus," "sin," "heaven," and "death" and color the right image when you hear them:

How many times did you hear "Jesus"? _____ "sin"? _____ "heaven"? _____ "death"? _____

Trace the sentence:

Talk about it: Who will live with God's people in heaven?

Look up: Revelation 21:1-4

WHERE IN THE BIBLE?

1. Circle the testament which the sermon was from:

   OLD TESTAMENT   NEW TESTAMENT

2. What book of the Bible was the sermon from?

   BOOK: _____

3. What chapter and verse was the sermon from?

   CHAPTER: _____   VERSES: _____ – _____

4. Draw a picture of something you need to do to obey God's Word:

GOD'S WORD IS
SWEETER THAN HONEY

Listen for the words "God," "Bible," and "cross" and color
the right image when you hear them:

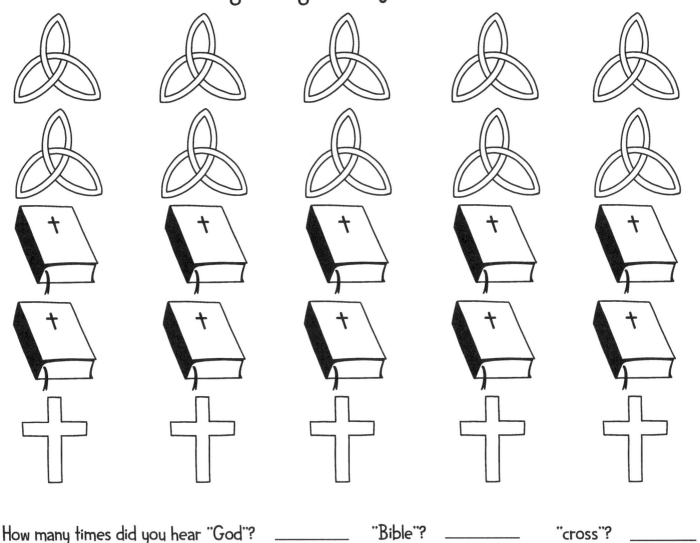

How many times did you hear "God"? _____ "Bible"? _____ "cross"? _____

**Trace the
sentence:**

Talk about it: What does it mean that God's Word is sweeter than honey?

Look up: Psalm 19:10

WHERE IN THE BIBLE?

1. Circle the testament which the sermon was from:

    OLD TESTAMENT   NEW TESTAMENT

2. What book of the Bible was the sermon from?

    BOOK: _____

3. What chapter and verse was the sermon from?

    CHAPTER: _____   VERSES: _____ – _____

4. Draw a picture of something you need to do to obey God's Word:

JESUS IS BUILDING HIS CHURCH

Listen for the words "Jesus," "sin," "church," and "God" and color

the right image when you hear them:

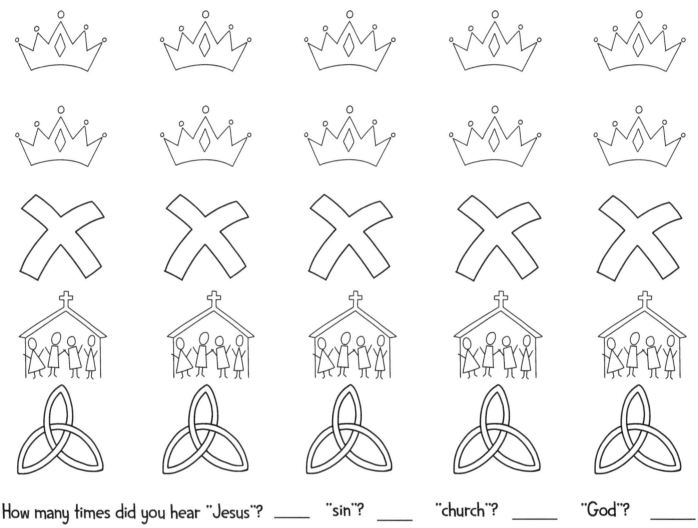

How many times did you hear "Jesus"? _____ "sin"? _____ "church"? _____ "God"? _____

Trace the

sentence:

Talk about it: What is the church made up of?

Look up: 1 Peter 2:4-4

WHERE IN THE BIBLE?

1. Circle the testament which the sermon was from:

OLD TESTAMENT   NEW TESTAMENT

2. What book of the Bible was the sermon from?

BOOK: _____

3. What chapter and verse was the sermon from?

CHAPTER: _____   VERSES: _____ – _____

4. Draw a picture of something you need to do to obey God's Word:

BELIEVE IN JESUS AND NEVER DIE

Listen for the words "Jesus," "cross," and "death" and color the right image when you hear them:

How many times did you hear "Jesus"? _____ "cross"? _____ "death"? _____

Trace the sentence:

Talk about it: Do you believe in Jesus?

Look up: John 11:25-26

WHERE IN THE BIBLE?

1. Circle the testament which the sermon was from:

OLD TESTAMENT   NEW TESTAMENT

2. What book of the Bible was the sermon from?

BOOK: _____

3. What chapter and verse was the sermon from?

CHAPTER: _____   VERSES: _____—_____

4. Draw a picture of something you need to do to obey God's Word:

TAKE UP YOUR CROSS AND FOLLOW JESUS

Listen for the words "Jesus," "cross," and "repent" and color

the right image when you hear them:

How many times did you hear "Jesus"? _____ "cross"? _____ "repent"? _____

Trace the

sentence:

Talk about it: What does it mean to take up your cross?

Look up: Matthew 16:23

WHERE IN THE BIBLE?

1. Circle the testament which the sermon was from:

   OLD TESTAMENT   NEW TESTAMENT

2. What book of the Bible was the sermon from?

   BOOK: _____

3. What chapter and verse was the sermon from?

   CHAPTER: _____   VERSES: _____ — _____

4. Draw a picture of something you need to do to obey God's Word:

WEEK 43

GOD'S FREE
GIFT IS ETERNAL LIFE

Listen for the words "God," "heaven," "cross," and "Bible" and color

the right image when you hear them:

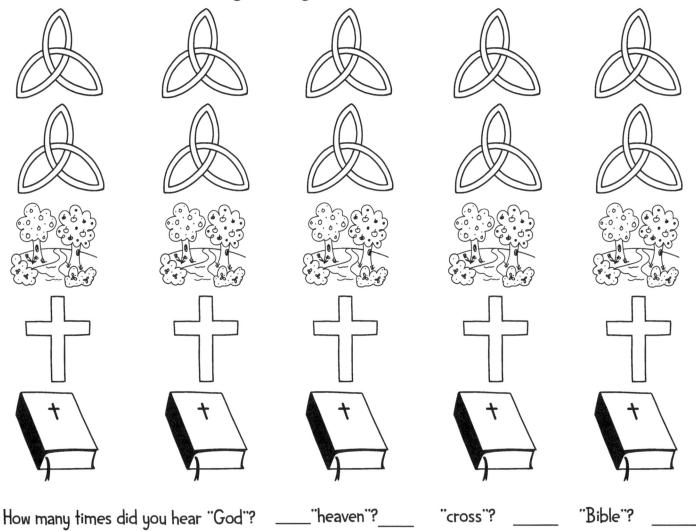

How many times did you hear "God"? _____ "heaven"? _____ "cross"? _____ "Bible"? _____

Trace the

sentence:

Talk about it: Who is this gift for?

Look up: Romans 3:22

WHERE IN THE BIBLE?

1. Circle the testament which the sermon was from:

OLD TESTAMENT   NEW TESTAMENT

2. What book of the Bible was the sermon from?

BOOK: _____

3. What chapter and verse was the sermon from?

CHAPTER: _____   VERSES: _____ — _____

4. Draw a picture of something you need to do to obey God's Word:

JESUS SITS AT GOD'S RIGHT HAND IN HEAVEN

Listen for the words "Jesus," "God," and "heaven" and color

the right image when you hear them:

How many times did you hear "Jesus"? _____   "God"? _____   "heaven"? _____

Trace the

sentence:

Talk about it: When did Jesus sit down beside God in heaven?

Look up: Hebrews 10:12

WHERE IN THE BIBLE?

1. Circle the testament which the sermon was from:

OLD TESTAMENT   NEW TESTAMENT

2. What book of the Bible was the sermon from?

BOOK: _____

3. What chapter and verse was the sermon from?

CHAPTER: _____   VERSES: _____ — _____

4. Draw a picture of something you need to do to obey God's Word:

The Holy Spirit Raised Jesus from the Dead

Listen for the words "Holy Spirit," "Jesus," and "death" and color the right image when you hear them:

How many times did you hear "Holy Spirit"? _____ "Jesus"? _____ "death"? _____

Trace the

sentence:

Talk about it: What does the Spirit do for Christians?

Look up: Romans 8:11

WHERE IN THE BIBLE?

1. Circle the testament which the sermon was from:

   OLD TESTAMENT   NEW TESTAMENT

2. What book of the Bible was the sermon from?

   BOOK: _____

3. What chapter and verse was the sermon from?

   CHAPTER: _____   VERSES: _____ – _____

4. Draw a picture of something you need to do to obey God's Word:

DO YOU LOVE GOD?

Listen for the words "God," "cross," "love," and "law" and color

the right image when you hear them:

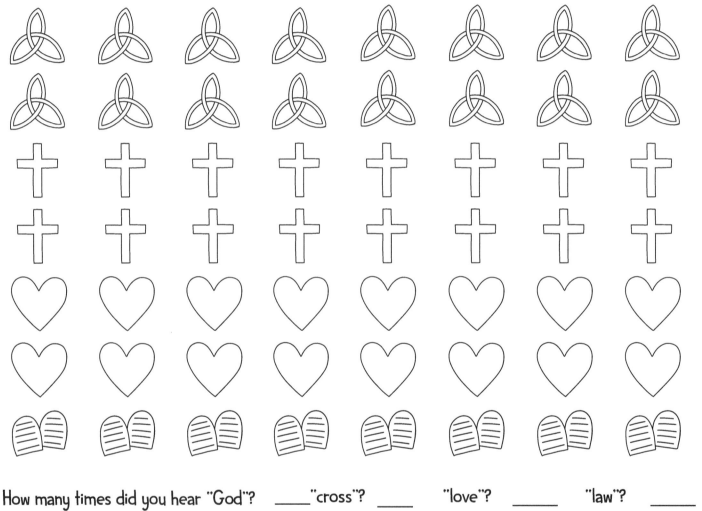

How many times did you hear "God"? _____ "cross"? _____ "love"? _____ "law"? _____

Trace the

sentence:

Talk about it: How do you know that you really love God?

Look up: 1 John 5:3

WHERE IN THE BIBLE?

1. Circle the testament which the sermon was from:

   OLD TESTAMENT   NEW TESTAMENT

2. What book of the Bible was the sermon from?

   BOOK: _____

3. What chapter and verse was the sermon from?

   CHAPTER: _____   VERSES: _____ – _____

4. Draw a picture of something you need to do to obey God's Word:

THE CHURCH IS JESUS' BRIDE

Listen for the words "Jesus," "sin," "church," and "heaven" and color the right image when you hear them:

How many times did you hear "Jesus"? ____ "sin"? ____ "church"? ____ "heaven"? ____

Trace the

sentence:

Talk about it: What did Jesus do for His bride?

Look up: Ephesians 5:25-27

WHERE IN THE BIBLE?

1. Circle the testament which the sermon was from:

    OLD TESTAMENT   NEW TESTAMENT

2. What book of the Bible was the sermon from?

    BOOK: _____

3. What chapter and verse was the sermon from?

    CHAPTER: _____   VERSES: _____ — _____

4. Draw a picture of something you need to do to obey God's Word:

REPENTANCE IS A GIFT

Listen for the words "Jesus," "Holy Spirit," "Bible," and "repent" and color the right image when you hear them:

How many times did you hear "Jesus"? _____ "Holy Spirit"? _____   "Bible"? _____   "repent"? _____

Trace the

sentence:

Talk about it: Who gives the gift of repentance?

Look up: Acts 5:30-31

WHERE IN THE BIBLE?

1. Circle the testament which the sermon was from:

    OLD TESTAMENT   NEW TESTAMENT

2. What book of the Bible was the sermon from?

    BOOK: _____

3. What chapter and verse was the sermon from?

    CHAPTER: _____   VERSES: _____ — _____

4. Draw a picture of something you need to do to obey God's Word:

GOD'S WORD HELPS
GOD'S PEOPLE GROW

Listen for the words "God," "Bible," "church," and "death" and color
the right image when you hear them:

How many times did you hear "God"? _____ "Bible"? _____ "church"? _____ "death"? _____

Trace the
sentence:

Talk about it: Why do God's people need to grow up?

Look up: Ephesians 4:13-14

WHERE IN THE BIBLE?

1. Circle the testament which the sermon was from:

OLD TESTAMENT   NEW TESTAMENT

2. What book of the Bible was the sermon from?

BOOK: _____

3. What chapter and verse was the sermon from?

CHAPTER: _____   VERSES: _____ — _____

4. Draw a picture of something you need to do to obey God's Word:

"Gospel" Means Good News

Listen for the words "Jesus," "cross," "love," and "heaven" and color
the right image when you hear them:

How many times did you hear "Jesus"? _____ "cross"? _____ "love"? _____ "heaven"? _____

Trace the

sentence:

Talk about it: Do all people teach the same gospel message?

Look up: Galatians 1:6-9

WHERE IN THE BIBLE?

1. Circle the testament which the sermon was from:

OLD TESTAMENT   NEW TESTAMENT

2. What book of the Bible was the sermon from?

BOOK: _____

3. What chapter and verse was the sermon from?

CHAPTER: _____   VERSES: _____ – _____

4. Draw a picture of something you need to do to obey God's Word:

GOD'S KINDNESS LEADS TO REPENTANCE

Listen for the words "God," "Holy Spirit," "cross," and "repent" and color

the right image when you hear them:

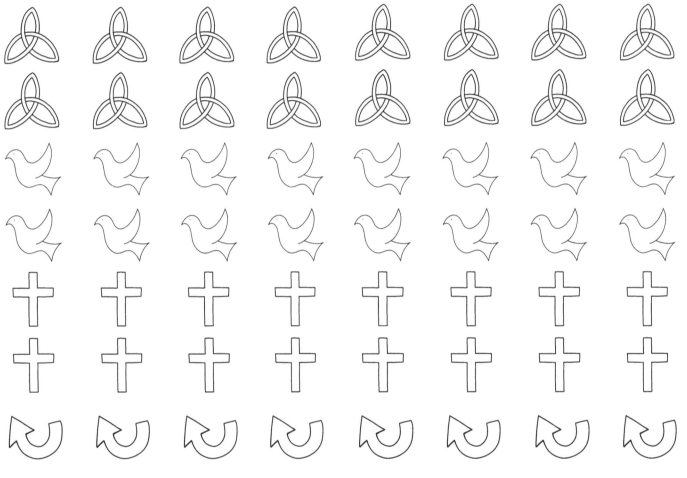

How many times did you hear "God"? _____ "Holy Spirit"? _____ "cross"? _____ "repent"? _____

Trace the

sentence:

Talk about it: How is God kind and patient to you?

Look up: Romans 2:4

WHERE IN THE BIBLE?

1. Circle the testament which the sermon was from:

OLD TESTAMENT   NEW TESTAMENT

2. What book of the Bible was the sermon from?

BOOK: _____

3. What chapter and verse was the sermon from?

CHAPTER: _____   VERSES: _____ — _____

4. Draw a picture of something you need to do to obey God's Word:

THE BIBLE IS ALL ABOUT JESUS

Listen for the words "Jesus," "Bible," "sin," and "church" and color
the right image when you hear them:

How many times did you hear "Jesus"? _____ "Bible"? _____   "sin"? _____   "church"? _____

Trace the
sentence:

Talk about it: Does the Old Testament talk about Jesus?

Look up: Luke 24:44-47

WHERE IN THE BIBLE?

1. Circle the testament which the sermon was from:

   OLD TESTAMENT   NEW TESTAMENT

2. What book of the Bible was the sermon from?

   BOOK: _____

3. What chapter and verse was the sermon from?

   CHAPTER: _____   VERSES: _____ — _____

4. Draw a picture of something you need to do to obey God's Word:

CPSIA information can be obtained
at www.ICGtesting.com
Printed in the USA
LVHW101813220620
658711LV00013B/1149